W9-CPW-056

The
Child's
World

Published by The Child's World®
1980 Lookout Drive • Mankato, MN 56003-1705
800-599-READ • www.childsworld.com

ACKNOWLEDGMENTS
The Child's World®: Mary Berendes, Publishing Director
The Design Lab: Design and page production
Red Line Editorial: Editorial direction

LIBRARY OF CONGRESS CATALOGING-IN-PUBLICATION DATA
Heinrichs, Ann.
  Similes and metaphors / by Ann Heinrichs ; illustrated by Dan
McGeehan and David Moore.
      p. cm.
  Includes bibliographical references and index.
  ISBN 978-1-60253-434-6 (library bound : alk. paper)
  1. Simile—Juvenile literature. 2. Metaphor—Juvenile literature. 3. Figures
of speech—Juvenile literature. 4. English language—Style—Juvenile
literature. I. McGeehan, Dan, ill. II. Moore, David, ill. III. Title.
  PE1445.S5H453 2010
  428.1—dc22   2010012346

Printed in the United States of America in Mankato, Minnesota.
March 2013
PA02180

ABOUT THE AUTHOR
Ann Heinrichs was lucky. Every year from
grade three through grade eight, she had a
big, fat grammar textbook and a grammar
workbook. She feels that this prepared her
for life. She is now the author of more than
100 books for children and young adults.
She has also enjoyed successful careers as
a children's book editor and an advertising
copywriter. Ann grew up in Fort Smith,
Arkansas, and lives in Chicago, Illinois.

ABOUT THE ILLUSTRATORS
Dan McGeehan spent his younger years
as an actor, author, playwright, cartoonist,
editor, and even as a casket maker. Now he
spends his days drawing little monsters!

David Moore is an illustration instructor
at a university who loves painting and
flying airplanes. Watching his youngest
daughter draw inspires David to illustrate
children's books.

My hair looks like a bird's nest.

TABLE OF CONTENTS

When a Bear Is Like a Ballerina

Once, a bear went ice-skating. The bear was graceful. He seemed to float along. His smile was sweet.

That story's okay. But isn't this next one more interesting?

The bear was as graceful as a ballerina. He seemed to float along like a butterfly. His smile was as sweet as honey.

What happened? We added **similes**:

as graceful as a ballerina

like a butterfly

as sweet as honey

Similes **compare** two things. Those two things are different in most ways. But they are alike in one surprising or important way.

Thing or person	Compared to	How both are surprisingly alike
bear	ballerina	Both are graceful.
bear	butterfly	Both float smoothly.
smile	honey	Both are sweet.

A simile is an interesting way of describing something. It can clear things up. It can make a story funny. After all, how could a bear ever be like a butterfly? Only in a simile!

7

As White As Snow

Some similes use the word as.

Mary had a little lamb.
Its fleece was white as snow.

My new blue blanket is
as soft as a kitten.

After the race, Claire's legs
were as limp as noodles.

Like a Log

Some similes use the word like. These similes usually answer the question "how?"

How did the dog sleep?
The dog slept like a log.

How fast did you run?
I ran like the wind.

Long Similes

A simile compares two things, but those things don't have to be objects. They can be entire activities, and they can take many words to explain.

Looking for my sister in the mall is like looking for a needle in a haystack.

I'm grounded all week. I feel like a bug trapped in a jar.

People swarmed around the movie star like ants near a box of doughnuts.

13

More Similes

We use similes all the time! Here are some more common similes:

as cool as a cucumber
as cute as a button
as easy as ABC
as flat as a pancake
as old as the hills
as smooth as silk

fits like a glove
spreads like wildfire
sleeps like a baby
sparkles like diamonds
sticks out like a sore thumb
grows like weeds

Simile Jokes

Similes can make good jokes. They compare things that are very different.

Q: How is a rabbit like a cornstalk?
A: They both have big ears.

Q: How is a baby like an old car?
A: They both have a rattle.

Q: How are pancakes like a baseball team?
A: They both need a good batter.

Do you know any other simile jokes?

My Mind's a Sponge

Her home is her castle.

That kid never stops eating.
He's a bottomless pit!

Those sisters are two peas in a pod.

In each example, the colored words create a **metaphor**. Metaphors are like similes. They compare two different things that are alike in one important way. However, a metaphor doesn't use *like* or *as*. In a metaphor, one thing just *is* something else.

Thing or person	Compared to	How they are alike
home	castle	Places where you are safe or in charge.
he	bottomless pit	Neither can be filled up.
sisters	two peas in a pod	They are very close and very similar.

Swim Like a Fish and Eat Like a Pig

Can you swim like a fish? Does your cousin eat like a pig? Similes and metaphors often use animals. We usually give animals certain **traits**. Whales are big, and pigs are messy or greedy. Sometimes the animals really have these traits. Sometimes they are untrue or **exaggerated**. Whales really are big, but pigs are actually quite clean.

Here are some more animals and their traits. Which ones do you think are exaggerated?

animal	traits in metaphors
chicken	fearful, cowardly
lion	brave
mule	stubborn
owl	wise
ox	strong
peacock	proud
weasel	sneaky

Life Is Just a Bowl of Cherries

Many songs and poems use metaphors. Some of those metaphors have become common sayings.

metaphor: You are my sunshine.
meaning: You are a bright spot in my life.

Do you know any songs or poems with metaphors or similes?

Life is a bowl of cherries!

That means life is fun!

How to Learn More

AT THE LIBRARY

Cleary, Brian P. *Skin Like Milk, Hair of Silk: What Are Similes and Metaphors?* Minneapolis, MN: Millbrook, 2009.

Juster, Norton. *As Silly As Knees, As Busy As Bees: An Astounding Assortment of Similes*. New York: HarperCollins, 1998.

Leedy, Loreen. *Crazy Like a Fox: A Simile Story*. New York: Holiday House, 2008.

McClarnon, Marciann. *Painless Junior Grammar*. Hauppauge, NY: Barron's Educational Series, 2007.

Schoolhouse Rock: Grammar Classroom Edition. Dir. Tom Warburton. Interactive DVD. Walt Disney, 2007.

ON THE WEB

Visit our home page for lots of links about grammar: *childsworld.com/links*

NOTE TO PARENTS, TEACHERS AND LIBRARIANS: We routinely check our Web links to make sure they're safe, active sites—so encourage your readers to check them out!

Glossary

compare (kum-PAIR): To notice what is the same and what is different between two or more things. Similes and metaphors compare different things.

exaggerated (eg-ZAJ-uh-rate-id): To make something more important or bigger than it really is. The traits of some animals are exaggerated in similes.

metaphor (MET-uh-fore): A way of describing something by saying it is something else. *You are my sunshine* is a metaphor.

similes (SIM-uh-leez): Ways of comparing things using *like* or *as*. *As cool as a cucumber* is a simile.

traits (TRATES): The qualities that make one thing different from another thing. One of a whale's traits is its large size.

(24)

Index